LOW CALORIE COMFORT

Recipes by

THE CALORIE DEFICIT QUEEN

All recipes and photography by
Kacy Allensworth

Copyright ©2022 Kacy Allensworth

About the Author

Kacy fully understands what it's like to struggle with weight and wellbeing. After years of yo-yo dieting, she dug deep into researching the science behind sustainable weight loss. Kacy and her husband lost a collective 130 lbs and ultimately became the best versions of themselves. It is her mission to help others with their personal health and weight loss journey.

Kacy currently resides in Texas with her husband and two little girls. Kacy spent 22 years in education and found a way to combine her passion for being an educator and her creativity in the kitchen. Kacy is a former personal trainer, director of fitness, and is a certified cognitive and nutrition coach.

Kacy would like to dedicate this book to her amazingly supportive husband, who took on extra duties so that she could pursue her passion, begin a social media account, and start a new career.

NOTES ABOUT...

Macros

The macros listed for each recipe is per serving size. These were calculated using the My Fitness Pal database for standard products. If you use alternate products or make substitutions, be mindful that the macro counts will likely change.

Spray oil

I recommend using avocado oil for its heart healthy benefits. You can sub any type of plant-based spray oil for any of the recipes. I do not include spray oil as additional calories in any of my recipes.

Cooking Times

Cooking time may vary based on size and type of pan or cooking vessel used. A few of these recipes make the use of an air fryer. If you do not own an air fryer you can use a conventional oven at the same temperature as noted in each recipe, and add a few minutes to the cooking time. Watch your food closely.

Optional Toppings

If a recipe includes optional toppings, these are not included in the calculation of the macros.

TABLE OF CONTENTS

Main Courses

Sides

Main Courses

6 servings

calories	fats(g)	carbs(g)	protein(g)
320	3	23	50

White Chicken Chili

Ingredients

2.25 lbs boneless skinless chicken breasts

1 4 oz can of diced green chilies

1 15 oz can cannellini beans

1 cup chopped white onion

1 32 oz container of chicken broth

1 tbsp garlic powder

1 tbsp cumin

1 tbsp dried oregano

1 cup fat free cottage cheese

1/4 cup cashew milk

salt & pepper to taste

Optional:

air fried corn tortilla strips

cilantro

light sour cream

Method

1. Add the undrained can of cannellini beans, green chilies, chopped white onion, garlic, cumin, and oregano to a crock pot. Stir all ingredients well.
2. Add the chicken breast to the crock pot and cover with the sauce/bean mixture.
3. Add all 32 oz of chicken broth to the crock pot. Cover the crockpot and cook on low 7 hours, or on high 4 hours.
4. When done, break up the chicken with two forks and stir into the chili.
5. Blend the cottage cheese and cashew milk in a blender for about 1 minute or until completely smooth.
6. Add the cottage cheese/milk mixture to the crockpot and stir to combine.
7. Salt and pepper the chili to taste.
8. Top with optional toppings such as cilantro, air fried tortilla strips, or light sour cream. Optional toppings are not in the calorie count.

4 servings

calories	fats(g)	carbs(g)	protein(g)
275	8	16	35

Buffalo Chicken Quesadilla

Ingredients

1 lb ground chicken

1/2 cup fat free cottage cheese

1/4 cup Franks red hot buffalo sauce

4 Ole Xtreme Wellness tortillas

8 slices Kraft Slim cut mozzarella cheese

Spray oil

Optional:

low calorie ranch dressing

Method

1. Heat a large skillet with light spray oil over medium high heat, and cook the ground chicken, breaking it up with a spoon until it is all browned and crumbly.
2. Add the fat free cottage cheese and Frank's red hot sauce to a blender and blend until smooth.
3. Pour the cottage cheese buffalo sauce into your pan of cooked ground chicken and stir until combined.
4. Heat a skillet pan over medium high heat on your stove. Lightly spray a tortilla with spray oil and add it to the pan oil side down.
5. Place one slice of slim cut mozzarella on one side of your tortilla. Top the cheese slice with 4 oz of the meat mixture, and then another slice of mozzarella.
6. Flip the bare half of the tortilla over the filling and cook for about 2 minutes until the bottom is golden and the cheese has started to melt. Then use a spatula to flip the half-moon quesadilla and continue to cook until all of the cheese is melted, and the underside is browned.
7. Remove the quesadilla to a cutting board and let the quesadilla sit for a minute before you slice into wedges. Repeat step 4-6 until all of the quesadillas are cooked.
8. Serve with low calorie ranch dressing. Optional toppings are not in the calorie count.

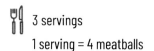

3 servings

1 serving = 4 meatballs

calories	fats(g)	carbs(g)	protein(g)
392	13	14	55

Chicken Parmesan
Meat Balls

Ingredients

1.25 lbs ground chicken (or 99% lean ground turkey)

2 tbsp chopped white onion

1 tsp chopped parsley

3 light rye Wasa crackers, processed into crumbs

1 clove garlic, minced

1/2 tbsp fennel seeds

zest of half a lemon

1/4 cup grated parmesan

1 egg, whisked

1 jar marinara sauce (I use Sal & Judy's)

spray oil

6 slices of Kraft slim cut mozzarella cheese

Method

1. Preheat your oven to 350F.

2. Place the first 9 ingredients, plus 2 tbsp of marinara sauce into a large bowl, and using your hands, gently mix together.

3. Shape into meatballs slightly larger than a golf ball. This recipe should make 12 meatballs. One serving is 4 meatballs.

4. Place the meatballs on a foil-lined baking sheet and spray the tops of the meatballs with spray oil.

5. Bake the meatballs on the center oven rack for 15 minutes.

6. Remove the meatballs from the oven and spoon 1 tbsp. of marinara sauce on top of each meatball.

7. Place 1/2 a slice of slim cut mozzarella cheese on top of each meatball.

8. Broil the meatballs in your oven for 3-5 minutes or until the cheese is golden and bubbly.

9. Remove the meatballs from the oven and serve warm.

calories	fats(g)	carbs(g)	protein(g)
286	6	15	43

Sesame Chicken

Ingredients

2 lbs boneless skinless chicken breasts

1 1/2 cups G Hugues Teriyaki marinade

1 tbsp garlic powder

1 tsp red pepper flakes

spray oil

4 cups frozen stir fry vegetables

Optional:

white rice

riced cauliflower

Sesame seeds

Method

1. Cut your chicken breasts into bite sized chunks.
2. Place the chicken into a large bowl with 1 cup of G Hughes Teriyaki marinade, 1 Tbsp of garlic powder, and 1 tsp of red pepper flakes. Stir to combine, cover and marinate for 1-2 hours or overnight in your refrigerator.
3. Lightly spray a nonstick frying pan with spray oil and place on medium-high heat.
4. Add the chicken (with the sauce it marinated in) to the frying pan. Cook for 7-8 minutes, turning two or three times during cooking until the chicken is well browned. The chicken should reach an internal temperature of 165 F.
5. Remove the cooked chicken from the pan and place in a bowl.
6. Add 4 cups of frozen stir fry vegetables to the hot pan and cook for 6-8 minutes or until heated thoroughly.
7. Return the cooked chicken to the pan of vegetables and add 1/2 cup of G Hughes teriyaki sauce. Stir to combine.
8. Serve the chicken and vegetables warm. Options include adding white rice, riced cauliflower, and/or sesame seeds.

calories	fats(g)	carbs(g)	protein(g)
465	17	31	47

2 servings (4 tacos each)

Mini Tacos

Ingredients

8 oz cooked chicken breasts, shredded

1/4 cup Bolthouse Farms Cilantro Avocado dressing

8 Mission Zero net carbs tortillas (25 calories each)

8 Kraft Slim cut mozzarella cheese slices

spray oil

toothpicks (to hold tacos closed)

Optional:

salsa

light sour cream

Method

1. Pre-heat your oven or air fryer to 400F.
2. Measure 8 oz of cooked chicken and shred using two forks or a food processor. A rotisserie chicken works great for this recipe.
3. Place the 8 oz of chicken in a large bowl and add the Bolthouse Cilantro Avocado dressing. Stir until all of the chicken is coated.
4. Place 8 tortillas flat on a foil-lined baking sheet and add 1 slice of slim cut mozzarella to each.
5. Using a standard sized cookie scoop, add a scoop of the chicken mixture to each tortilla. This should be about 1 oz of chicken per tortilla.
6. Fold each tortilla in half creating half-moon shapes, and use a toothpick to pierce through both sides, holding the tacos closed.
7. Lightly spray the tacos with spray oil and bake or air fry at 400F. They will need to bake in an oven for 13 - 15 minutes and in an air fryer for 6-8 minutes.
8. Remove the tacos from the oven or air fryer and serve with the optional toppings. Optional toppings are not included in the calories.

10

calories	fats(g)	carbs(g)	protein(g)
328	8	8	56

Buffalo Chicken Meatballs

Ingredients

1.10 lbs ground chicken breast (or 99% lean ground turkey)

2 light rye Wasa crackers, processed into crumbs

1/4 cup carrots processed into very fine pieces

1/4 tsp salt

1/4 tsp pepper

3 tbsp Egg Beaters (or egg whites)

2 tbsp Franks Red Hot sauce + sauce for tossing with cooked meatballs

Optional:

Bolthouse blue cheese dressing

green onions

Method

1. Preheat your oven to 400F.
2. Place the first 6 ingredients + 2 tbsp Frank's Red Hot sauce into a large bowl, and using your hands, gently mix together.
3. Using a standard sized cookie scoop, place meatballs onto a foil-lined baking sheet. The cookie scoop helps with making all the meatballs the same size. Roll the meatballs between the palm of your hands to create a more round shape. This recipe should make 20 meatballs. One serving is 10 meatballs.
4. Place the pan of meatballs in the oven at 400F and bake for 15 minutes.
5. Remove from the oven and place the cooked meatballs in a medium sized bowl. Toss the meatballs in additional amount of desired Franks Red Hot sauce. Optional toppings include blue cheese dressing and green onions. Optional toppings are not included in the calories.
6. Serve warm.

calories	fats(g)	carbs(g)	protein(g)
250	5	19	32

Grilled Chicken Burger

Ingredients

16 oz ground chicken (or 16 oz 99% lean ground turkey)

1 tsp garlic powder

1 tsp onion powder

1/2 tsp chili powder

1/2 tsp paprika

1/2 tbsp Swerve brown sugar

1 tsp salt

1 tsp pepper

1/4 cup diced red bell pepper (30g)

1/4 cup diced yellow onion (30g)

Keto Culture hamburger buns

Method

1. Place your ground chicken into a large mixing bowl. Add all of the spices from the garlic powder to the pepper. Add the diced red bell pepper and yellow onion.
2. Using a large spoon or your hands, incorporate the spices, bell pepper and onion into your ground meat.
3. Slightly wet your hands and scoop out 1/4 of the meat mixture and then create the patty in your palms. Flatten them until they are 1/2 inch thick. Repeat 3 more times.
4. Grill ground chicken burgers at 375F over direct heat for around 4 minutes on each side.
5. Remove the chicken burgers from the grill and transfer to a large plate. Let rest for around 5 minutes.
6. Place your burger in a low calorie bun and dress your burger as desired. All dressing options will add calories to your burger.

calories	fats(g)	carbs(g)	protein(g)
295	7	18	40

Pulled Pork Sandwiches

Ingredients

2 lbs boneless lean pork loin

1 tsp salt

1 tsp pepper

2 tsp minced garlic

1/2 cup broth (beef or chicken)

1 tsp liquid smoke

1/2 bottle (18 tbsp.) G Huges Mesquite BBQ sauce

Keto Culture hamburger buns

Optional:

sliced red cabbage

pickle slices

Method

1. Add the pork, salt, pepper, minced garlic, broth and liquid smoke to a crockpot.
2. Cover and cook on low for 8 hours or on high for 4 hours.
3. When done, break up the pork with two forks.
4. Add half of a bottle of G Hughes BBQ sauce and stir to combine.
5. Serve 5 oz of the pork per sandwich on a low calorie bun or bread and add optional toppings as desired. Optional toppings are not included in the calories.

13

4 servings

calories	fats(g)	carbs(g)	protein(g)
245	9	11	29

Air fried Salmon with Mango Salsa

Ingredients

4 frozen salmon filets (~7 oz each)

2 tbsp Dijon mustard

4 tbsp sugar free maple syrup

1 tsp garlic powder

spray oil

Mango Salsa

1 cup diced fresh mango

1 cup diced grape tomatoes

1/4 cup finely diced red onion

1 diced jalapeno

Juice of 1/2 lime

Method

1. Preheat your air fryer to 375F.

2. Spray your air fryer basket with spray oil.

3. Place the frozen salmon in the air fryer basket and cook for 7-8 minutes.

4. In a small bowl, mix the Dijon mustard, sugar free maple syrup and garlic powder.

5. Open the air fryer basket and baste the top with the mustard mixture, flip, then baste the other side. Air fry for an additional 7-8 minutes.

6. In a medium sized bowl, combine all mango salsa ingredients together.

7. Remove the cooked salmon from the air fryer, top with the 1/4 of the mango salsa and serve.

2 servings

calories	fats(g)	carbs(g)	protein(g)
446	10	25	64

Chicken Parmesan

Ingredients

2 split chicken breasts (8 oz each), pounded thin

4 Light Rye Wasa crackers

2 tsp grated parmesan

1 tsp salt

pepper to taste

1 tsp dried oregano

1/4 cup egg whites

1/2 cup low calorie pasta sauce

2 slices Kraft slim cut mozzarella

2-3 zucchini

spray oil

Optional:

fresh basil

Method

1. Preheat your oven to 400F.
2. Process the 4 Wasa crackers in a blender or food processer until you get fine crumbs. Pour the crumbs onto a shallow plate.
3. Add the parmesan, salt, pepper, and oregano to the cracker crumbs. Mix with a fork to combine.
4. To a second shallow plate, add 1/4 cup of egg whites.
5. One at a time, dip the chicken breasts into the egg whites covering both sides of the chicken, and then into the bread crumb mixture pressing the breadcrumbs into the chicken.
6. Set a shallow frying pan on medium-high heat on the stove and spray with spray oil. Sear the chicken on both sides, browning the bread crumb exterior. This will take about 1- 2 minutes per side.
7. Place the seared chicken onto a parchment paper lined baking sheet and into the oven for 10 minutes or until the chicken reaches an internal temp of 165F.
8. Remove the chicken from the oven and spoon 1/4 cup of pasta sauce onto the tops of each chicken breast. Place 1 slice of slim cut mozzarella on top of the pasta sauce.
9. Place the chicken back into the oven for 3-4 minutes or until the cheese is melted.
10. Using a vegetable spiraler, spiral cut 4 cups of zucchini. Plate 2 cups of raw zoodles (zucchini noodles) per serving. You can also purchase pre-made frozen zoodles.
11. Remove the chicken from the oven and serve warm over the zoodles.
12. Top with basil as an optional topping. Optional toppings are not included in the calorie count.

4 servings

calories	fats(g)	carbs(g)	protein(g)
278	2	25	40

Shrimp Kabobs with Peanut Sauce

Ingredients

1.5 lbs fresh shrimp

salt and pepper to taste

1 tbsp garlic powder

1 red bell pepper

1 green bell pepper

1 yellow onion

1 fresh pineapple

Peanut sauce:

3/4 cup G Hughes sweet chili sauce

1/4 cup soy sauce

1/4 cup PB2 or PB fit powder

2-4 tbsp water (to thin sauce)

Optional:

Sriracha

Method

1. Peel and devein the fresh shrimp. Rinse with cold water.
2. Season the shrimp with salt, pepper and garlic powder.
3. Soak 12 wooden skewers in a pan of water for a minimum of 30 minutes.
4. Chop the green and red bell pepper and onion into 1.5 inch sized pieces.
5. Cut the fresh pineapple into large 1.5 - 2 inch chunks.
6. Remove the wooden sticks from the water and skewer each wooden stick with 3 shrimp pieces, one red bell pepper piece, one green bell pepper piece, a yellow onion piece and a pineapple chunk. Alternate the order of pieces as you like.
7. Preheat your grill or a grill pan to medium high heat. Cook the kabobs for 2-3 minutes per side, or until shrimp are pink and opaque and vegetables are tender.
8. To make the peanut sauce combine all ingredients in a small bowl and mix well. Divide the peanut sauce into 4 servings to be used for dipping sauce.
9. Add sriracha to the peanut sauce as an optional topping.

16

4 servings

calories	fats(g)	carbs(g)	protein(g)
405	8	47	36

Creamy Chicken Alfredo

Ingredients

2 lbs boneless skinless chicken breasts

salt & pepper

2 tsp garlic powder

8 oz protein pasta (I use Barilla penne)

1/3 cup white onion chopped

2 tsp minced garlic

1 tbsp cornstarch

1 cup unsweetened cashew milk

1 tsp onion powder

6 Laughing Cow light wedges

1/2 cup chicken broth

Optional:

basil

parmesan

Method

1. Cut your chicken breasts into strips and season with salt, pepper and garlic powder.
2. Lightly spray a nonstick frying pan with spray oil and place on medium-high heat.
3. Add the chicken to the frying pan. Cook for 7-8 minutes, turning two or three times during cooking until well browned. The chicken should reach an internal temperature of 165F.
4. Remove the cooked chicken from the pan and place in a bowl.
5. Cook 8 oz of pasta according to the directions on the box.
6. Add the chopped onion and minced garlic to the same pan you cooked the chicken in. Sauté for 1-2 minutes, then add the cornstarch and stir.
7. Add the cashew milk and onion powder and stir until there are no cornstarch lumps.
8. Add the 6 wedges of Laughing Cow light and 1/2 cup of chicken broth. Stir with a spoon or whisk for 5-6 minutes or until the cheese is melted and the sauce thickens. Note: this alfredo sauce will be brownish in color.
9. Add the cooked chicken and cooked pasta to your alfredo sauce and stir.
10. Top with optional toppings such as fresh basil or parmesan. Optional toppings are not included in the calorie count.

calories	fats(g)	carbs(g)	protein(g)
335	3	28	50

Double Decker Tuna Burger

Ingredients

17 oz can tuna (in water) drained

1 celery stalk, diced (30g)

1/8 red bell pepper, diced (25g)

1 tbsp Dijon mustard

2 tbsp plain nonfat Greek yogurt

1 tsp dill

1 tsp dried parsley

salt and pepper to taste

2 tbsp egg whites

2 light rye Wasa crackers, processed into fine crumbs

spray oil

Low calorie bun (I use Keto Culture)

Optional:

lettuce, tomato, red onion

Method

1. Preheat your air fryer to 400F.
2. In a medium bowl, combine the tuna, diced celery, diced red bell pepper, Dijon mustard, Greek yogurt, dill, parsley, salt, pepper, and egg whites. Mix well to combine.
3. Add the processed Wasa cracker crumbs to the same bowl and use your hands to combine. Shape the mixture into two round patties.
4. Spray your air fryer basket with spray oil and air fry at 400F for 12-15 minutes.
5. Remove the tuna burgers from the air fryer and serve on a low-calorie bun.
6. Add optional toppings to dress your burger. Optional toppings are not included in the calorie count.

calories	fats(g)	carbs(g)	protein(g)
380	5	29	55

BBQ Chicken Pizza

Ingredients

Joseph's Lavash bread (large)

1/4 cup G Hughes Mesquite BBQ sauce

4 oz grilled or rotisserie chicken, chopped

1/4 cup red onion cut into thin slices

1/2 cup Fat free Mozzarella shredded cheese

2 tbsp cilantro chopped

Optional:

2 tbsp Bolthouse ranch dressing

Method

1. Preheat the oven to 350F.
2. Place 1 Lavash bread on a sheet pan lined with parchment paper and bake for 5 minutes.
3. Remove from the oven and spread the BBQ sauce evenly on top of the Lavash bread.
4. Add 4oz of chopped chicken breast, red onion slices and mozzarella cheese to the top of your pizza.
5. Bake your pizza for 8-10 minutes.
6. Remove from the oven and top with cilantro.
7. Add optional ranch dressing topping as desired. Optional toppings are not included in the calorie count.

2 servings

calories	fats(g)	carbs(g)	protein(g)
379	5	32	52

Cheesy Chicken Burritos

Ingredients

8 oz precooked chicken breast, shredded

2 Olé Wellness tortilla wraps

1/2 cup fat free cottage cheese

1/2 packet (1.25 oz) taco seasoning

2 tbsp cashew milk

1/4 cup fat free shredded mozzarella cheese

1/2 cup cannellini beans

spray oil

Optional:

salsa

nonfat yogurt

Method

1. Cut your chicken breasts into bite sized chunks.
2. Add the cottage cheese, taco seasoning and cashew milk to a blender. Blend until completely smooth, about 1-2 minutes.
3. Place the chicken into a large bowl and add the cottage cheese mixture, mozzarella cheese and cannellini beans. Stir until combined.
4. Divide the chicken mixture among two tortillas. Wrap burrito style.
5. Heat a nonstick frying pan or griddle on the stove on medium - high heat and lightly spray with spray oil.
6. Place the burritos seam side down and cook for 2-3 minutes or until browned. Flip the burrito and brown the other side for 1-2 minutes.
7. Transfer to a plate and serve warm.
8. Add optional toppings such as salsa or nonfat yogurt as desired. Optional toppings are not included in the calorie count.

calories	fats(g)	carbs(g)	protein(g)
301	5	38	26

Creamy Cajun Pasta with Turkey

Ingredients

8 oz precooked turkey breasts, chopped

salt & pepper

Cajun seasoning blend to taste

6 oz penne pasta (I use either Barilla or Banza)

200g brussels sprouts, shredded

100g green bell pepper, thinly sliced

100g red bell pepper, thinly sliced

100g yellow onion, thinly sliced

6 Laughing Cow light wedges

1/2 cup chicken broth

spray oil

Method

1. Cook the pasta according to the directions on the box.
2. Place a large pan on medium high heat on your stove and spray with spray oil. Sautee the onion, red bell peppers, and green bell peppers for about 4-5 minutes or until softened. Salt and pepper the vegetables while sauteing.
3. Add the shredded brussels sprouts to the same pan and sauté for an additional 2 minutes.
4. Add the cooked turkey breasts, Laughing Cow wedges and 1/2 cup chicken broth to the pan. Turn the stove to medium heat and cover for 4 minutes.
5. Uncover, add the cooked and drained pasta and stir until the cheese is melted and combined.
6. Season with Cajun seasoning to taste.
7. Serve warm.

calories	fats(g)	carbs(g)	protein(g)
281	8	15	38

Stuffed Peppers

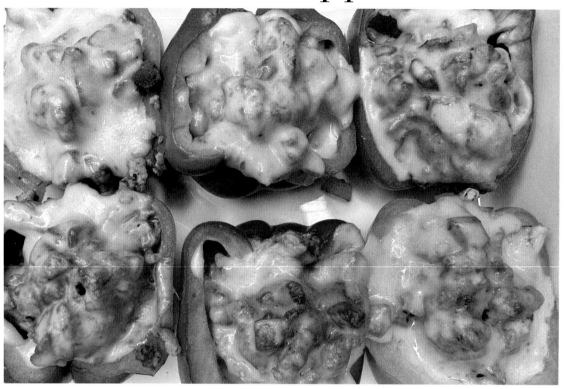

Ingredients

1 lb ground chicken breast (or 99% lean ground turkey)

Spray oil

1/2 cup diced white onion

2 tbsp tomato paste

2 tsp garlic, minced

1 14 oz can diced tomatoes, drained

1 tsp Italian seasoning

salt & pepper to taste

1/2 cup fat free shredded mozzarella

4 Bell peppers (I used 2 green, 1 red, and 1 orange)

8 slices Kraft slim cut mozzarella cheese

Method

1. Preheat your oven to 400F.
2. In a large skillet, over medium heat, add spray oil and cook the chopped onion until soft, about 3 minutes. Stir in the minced garlic and tomato paste and cook until fragrant, about 1 minute.
3. Add the ground chicken and using a wooden spoon, break up the meat and cook until browned.
4. Stir in the drained diced tomatoes, Italian seasoning, and salt and pepper to taste. Cook for 3 - 4 minutes allowing any juices to evaporate.
5. Remove the pan from the stove and stir in a 1/2 cup of shredded mozzarella.
6. Cut your peppers length wise, clear out any seeds, and place them cut side up in a rectangular baking dish.
7. Spoon chicken mixture into each bell pepper. top each with 1 slice of slim cut mozzarella.
8. Cover the baking dish with foil and bake until peppers are tender, about 30 minutes.
9. Remove the peppers from the oven and top each with 1/2 slice of slim cut mozzarella.
10. Uncover the dish and continue to bake until the cheese is browned and bubbly, about an additional 8 minutes.
11. Remove from the oven and serve warm.

calories	fats(g)	carbs(g)	protein(g)
208	2	5	42

Parmesan Crusted Cod

Ingredients

4 fresh cod fillets (6 oz each)

3 light rye Wasa crackers, processed into fine crumbs

1 tsp garlic powder

2 tsp grated parmesan cheese

1 tsp dried parsley

salt & pepper

spray oil

1 lemon

Method

1. Preheat your oven to 425F.
2. In a medium bowl, combine 1/4 cup of light rye Wasa cracker crumbs with garlic powder, parmesan cheese, parsley and the zest of half a lemon.
3. Arrange the cod fillets on a baking sheet lined with parchment paper and season with salt and pepper.
4. Divide the bread crumb mixture among the 2 cod fillets, pressing lightly so that it adheres.
5. Lightly spray the tops of the fillets and bread crumb topping with spray oil.
6. Place the fish in the oven and bake for 10-12 minutes, or until the top is lightly browned and the fish is mostly opaque (just cooked through). Keep in mind that the cooking time will depend on the thickness of your fillets.
7. Remove from the oven and serve warm.

4 servings

calories	fats(g)	carbs(g)	protein(g)
462	14	46	38

Triple Taco Stack

Ingredients

1.25 lbs ground chicken breast (or 99% lean ground turkey)

spray oil

1/2 packet (1.25 oz) taco seasoning

1 16 oz can fat free refried beans

1 16 oz bag of shredded ice burg lettuce

1 container of pre-made pico de gallo

1 pkg Mission tostada shells (you will need 12 tostada shells)

Optional:

Bolthouse cilantro avocado dressing

light sour cream

Method

1. Heat a large skillet with light spray oil over medium high heat, and cook the ground chicken, breaking it up with a spoon until it is all browned and crumbly.

2. Add 1/2 packet of taco seasoning to the pan and 1/4 cup of water. Stir to combine and allow the water to evaporate for about 2-3 minutes.

3. Heat the refried beans in a small microwavable bowl for 2 minutes or in a saucepan for 3-5 minutes on medium heat stirring frequently.

4. Layer one tostada shell with 2 tbsp. of refried beans, 1.5 oz of taco meat, 1/3 cup of shredded lettuce and 1 tbsp of pico de gallo. Repeat these layers two more times to complete 1 taco stack.

5. Repeat step 4 to make additional taco stacks.

6. Add optional toppings such as light sour cream or Bolthouse dressing. Optional toppings are not included in the calorie count.

4 servings

calories	fats(g)	carbs(g)	protein(g)
465	7	54	47

Coconut Curry Shrimp

Ingredients

1.5 lbs of fresh shrimp

1 cup jasmine rice, dry

1 cup yellow onion, diced (150g)

2 cups carrots, thinly sliced (250g)

1 13.5 oz can light coconut milk

24 oz chicken broth

1 tbsp curry powder

2 tsp minced garlic

2 tsp minced ginger

1/2 tbsp turmeric

salt and pepper to taste

1 tbsp corn starch

spray oil

Optional:

sriracha

parsley

Method

1. Peel and devein the fresh shrimp. Rinse with cold water.

2. In a medium saucepan, over medium heat, bring 1 cup of jasmine rice and 2 cups of chicken broth to a boil. Season with salt, lower heat to simmer, cover and cook for 18 minutes or until rice is tender and all broth is absorbed.

3. In a large skillet on medium-high heat, add spray oil, diced yellow onion and sliced carrots. Cook for about 4-5 minutes or until the vegetables start to turn tender.

4. Turn the heat to medium and add the minced garlic, minced ginger, curry powder and turmeric to the vegetables and stir 1-2 minutes or until fragrant.

5. Add 1 cup of chicken broth and can of light coconut milk to the vegetables. Stir to combine and bring to a light boil. Then turn heat to lowest setting, place a lid on the pan and allow to simmer for 5-6 minutes.

6. In a small bowl, whisk 1 tbsp of cornstarch with 1/4 cup of water. Add this mixture to your pan, stir and allow the sauce to thicken.

7. Add the shrimp to the pan, turn the heat back to medium, cover with a lid and allow the shrimp to cook 4-5 minutes or until the shrimp is pink. Uncover and salt and pepper to taste.

8. Serve the curried shrimp and vegetables with 1/2 cup of cooked jasmine rice.

9. Additional toppings such as sriracha and parsely are optional. Optional toppings are not included in the calorie count.

4 servings

calories	fats(g)	carbs(g)	protein(g)
188	7	5	26

Skillet Pork Chops with Gravy

Ingredients

4 boneless pork chops (4 oz each)

2 tbsp I Can't Believe it's Not Butter Light

1/2 cup yellow onion, diced

1 tsp garlic powder

1 tsp onion powder

1 tsp smoked paprika

1/2 tsp sage

1 cup chicken broth

1 tbsp white wine vinegar

1 tbsp corn starch

salt and pepper to taste

parsley

spray oil

Method

1. Season the pork chops with salt, pepper, smoked paprika and sage.
2. Heat a large skillet on medium-high heat and spray with spray oil.
3. Cook the pork chops for 2-3 minutes on each side or until golden brown.
4. Reduce the heat to low and cover the skillet with a lid. Cook for 6-8 minutes or until the chops reach an internal temperature of 145F.
5. Remove the pork chops from the skillet and set aside.
6. Set the temperature to medium and add the butter and diced onion to the skillet. Cook for about 3-4 minutes or until the onion is tender.
7. Add the chicken broth, white wine vinegar, garlic powder and onion powder to the skillet. Using a wooden spoon, break up any bits of food at the bottom of the skillet.
8. In a small bowl whisk 1 tbsp of corn starch with 1/4 cup water. Add the corn starch mixture to the pan and stir to combine. Set the temperature to low and allow the sauce to reduce and thicken.
9. Remove the skillet from the heat, add the cooked pork chops back to the pan and spoon the gravy over each pork chop.
10. Top with fresh parsley and serve warm. I served the porkchops with rice and roasted sweet potatoes as sides.

calories	fats(g)	carbs(g)	protein(g)
324	4	34	37

Chicken Tortilla Soup

Ingredients

3 boneless skinless chicken breasts (24 oz)

1 cup white onion, diced

1 (14 oz) can black beans

1 (14 oz) can corn

1 (28 oz) can diced tomatoes

1 (4 oz) can diced green chilies

1 packet taco seasoning

4 cups chicken broth

4 tbsp cilantro

1 12 oz can fat free evaporated milk

salt and pepper to taste

2 limes

Optional:

shredded cheese

sour cream

air fried tortilla strips

Method

1. Season boneless chicken breast with salt and pepper to taste. Arrange in a single layer in a 6-qt slow cooker.
2. Add onions, black beans, corn, diced tomatoes, diced green chilies, and taco seasoning.
3. Add chicken broth and stir to combine.
4. Cover with lid and cook on HIGH for about 4 to 5 hours or on LOW for about 6 to 7 hours until chicken is cooked and easily shreds.
5. Remove chicken and coarsely shred with two forks. Return to pot and continue to cook for another 3 to 5 minutes or until meat is heated through. Season with salt and pepper, if needed.
6. Add the can of evaporated milk and stir to combine.
7. Ladle soup into serving bowls and top with cilantro and a squeeze of lime.
8. Additional toppings such as shredded cheese, sour cream and air fried tortilla strips can be added. Optional toppings are not included in the calorie count.

2 servings

calories	fats(g)	carbs(g)	protein(g)
345	7	17	54

Grilled Tuna Steak

Ingredients

2 tuna steaks (8 oz each)

3 tbsp soy sauce

2 tbsp Swerve brown sugar

1 tbsp chili paste

1 tbsp extra virgin olive oil

1 tsp garlic powder

Method

1. In a medium bowl, mix the soy sauce, olive oil, brown sugar, garlic powder and chili paste with a whisk.
2. Place the tuna steaks in the marinade, cover and marinate in the refrigerator for 30 minutes to overnight.
3. Preheat an outdoor grill on high and lightly oil the grate.
4. Remove the tuna steaks from the marinade and shake off excess. Reserve marinade for basting.
5. Cook the tuna steaks on the preheated grill for 5-6 minutes; flip each and baste with reserved marinade. Cook for an additional 5 minutes or to desired doneness. Discard any remaining marinade.
6. Serve warm. I typically serve this dish with roasted broccoli.

4 servings

calories	fats(g)	carbs(g)	protein(g)
420	8	40	47

Green Chili Chicken Enchiladas

Ingredients

14 oz cooked chicken breasts

3/4 cup nonfat Greek yogurt

3/4 cup green salsa

12 Mission super soft white corn tortillas

1 cup green enchilada sauce

1 cup fat free shredded mozzarella

spray oil

Method

1. Preheat your oven to 350F.
2. Shred the cooked chicken breasts with 2 forks or a food processor.
3. In a medium bowl, mix the chicken breast pieces with Greek yogurt and green salsa.
4. Divide the chicken mixture evenly among 12 tortillas and roll into enchiladas.
5. Place seam side down in an 8x8 baking dish and pour 1 cup of enchilada sauce over the tortillas covering them.
6. Top the enchiladas with shredded mozzarella, cover the dish with foil and place in the oven for 25-30 minutes.
7. Uncover and broil for 5 additional minutes or until the cheese is browned and bubbly.
8. Remove from oven and serve warm. I typically serve this dish with a side salad.

4 servings

calories	fats(g)	carbs(g)	protein(g)
390	5	52	41

Eggroll in a Bowl

Ingredients

20 oz ground chicken (1.25 lbs)

Spray oil

2 14 oz bags of Dole Classic Coleslaw

1/2 cup G Hughes Stir Fry sauce

1 1/2 tsp garlic powder

1 1/2 tbsp minced ginger

salt & pepper

1 cup jasmine rice, dry

2 cups chicken broth

Optional:

Everything Bagel Seasoning

green onions

sriracha sauce

Method

1. In a medium saucepan, over medium heat, bring 1 cup of jasmine rice and 2 cups of chicken broth to a boil. Lower heat to simmer, cover and cook for 18 minutes or until rice is tender and all broth is absorbed.

2. Place a large, deep-frying pan on your stove on medium-high heat. Once heated, spray the pan with spray oil and add your ground chicken.

3. Cook the ground chicken, breaking it up with a spoon until it is all browned and crumbly.

4. Add the two bags of coleslaw to your pan and stir for about 5-6 minutes, or until the cabbage is soft and wilted.

5. Add a half cup of stir fry sauce, garlic powder, and minced ginger to the pan. Stir and simmer for an additional 4-5 minutes.

6. Season to taste with salt and pepper.

7. Serve warm with 1/2 cup of cooked rice.

8. Top with everything bagel seasoning, green onions or sriracha sauce if desired. Optional toppings are not included in the calorie count.

30

4 servings

calories	fats(g)	carbs(g)	protein(g)
256	5	26	33

Buffalo Chicken Sandwich

Ingredients

4 split chicken breasts (4 oz each),
pounded thin

6 Light Rye Wasa crackers

1 tsp salt

pepper to taste

1/4 cup egg whites

1/2 cup Franks Red Hot buffalo sauce

4 large lettuce leaves

4 slices tomato

Keto Culture buns

Spray oil

Optional:

Blue cheese or ranch dressing

Method

1. Preheat your oven to 400F.
2. Process 6 Wasa crackers in a blender or food processer until you get fine crumbs. Pour the crumbs onto a shallow plate.
3. Add salt and pepper to the cracker crumbs. Mix with a fork to combine.
4. Add 1/4 cup of egg whites to a clean shallow plate.
5. One at a time, dip the chicken breasts into the egg whites covering both sides of the chicken, and then into the bread crumb mixture pressing the breadcrumbs into the chicken.
6. Set a shallow frying pan on medium-high heat on the stove and spray with spray oil. Sear the chicken on both sides, browning the bread crumb exterior. This will take about 1- 2 minutes per side.
7. Place the seared chicken onto a parchment paper lined baking sheet and into the oven for 10 minutes.
8. Place 1/2 cup of Frank's Red Hot Sauce onto a shallow plate. Remove the chicken from the oven and dredge the chicken in the Red Hot Sauce.
9. Serve the chicken warm with bun, lettuce and a tomato slice.
10. Add optional toppings such as blue cheese or ranch dressing as desired. Optional toppings are not included in the calorie count. I typically serve this with carrot fries.

SIDES

calories	fats(g)	carbs(g)	protein(g)
86	1	18	2

Carrot Fries

Ingredients

380 g carrot sticks

Seasoning of your choice

*I use DanO's and ranch seasoning

Spray oil

Method

1. Preheat your air frier to 400F.
2. Place your carrot sticks in a bowl and top with seasoning of your choice. Place the seasoned carrot sticks in your air fryer basket and spray lightly with spray oil. You may need to cook the carrot sticks in two batches depending on the size of your air fryer.
3. Air fry for 10 minutes, remove the basket and give a quick shake, then cook an additional 5 minutes or until crispy and tender on the inside.
4. Serve immediately.

calories	fats(g)	carbs(g)	protein(g)
72	3	4	7

Roasted Broccoli

Ingredients

8 cups fresh broccoli florets (~700g)

1 tbsp garlic powder

1 tsp salt

1/2 tsp pepper

1/4 cup grated parmesan cheese

spray oil

Method

1. Preheat your oven to 425F.
2. In a large bowl add your broccoli florets and spray generously with spray oil.
3. Add the garlic powder, salt, pepper and parmesan cheese to the broccoli and mix until combined.
4. Line a baking sheet with foil and spread your broccoli florets evenly onto the baking sheet.
5. Sprinkle any leftover seasoning mixture atop the broccoli.
6. Bake on the center rack of your oven for 20-22 minutes.
7. Remove from the oven and serve warm.

2 servings

calories	fats(g)	carbs(g)	protein(g)
52	1	8	3

Simple Side Salad

Ingredients

4 cups of spring mix

16 grape tomatoes

1/2 a cucumber, sliced

Optional:

Dressing of your choice

Method

1. Plate 2 cups of spring mix per person.
2. Add 8 grape tomatoes and 1/4 a cup of sliced cucumber to each plate.
3. Top with your favorite low calorie dressing. The salad dressing is not included in the calorie count.

***Note: The reason I included such a simple recipe in this cookbook was because this is a weekly addition to many of my meals and I wanted this e-book to be authentic to the types of meals and side dishes I typically consume.

4 servings

calories	fats(g)	carbs(g)	protein(g)
118	1	25	2

Roasted Sweet Potatos

Ingredients

2 large sweet potatoes (500g)

spray oil

1/2 tbsp salt

1 tsp pepper

1/2 tbsp Swerve brown sugar

1/2 tsp chili powder

1 tsp garlic powder

1 tsp smoked paprika

Method

1. Preheat your oven to 425F.
2. Cut the sweet potatoes into 1/2 inch cubes.
3. In a small bowl, mix together the salt, pepper, brown sugar, chili powder, garlic powder and paprika.
4. Place the cubed sweet potatoes into a large bowl and spray generously with spray oil.
5. Add the spice mixture and toss with the sweet potatoes to coat.
6. Line a baking sheet with foil and spread your sweet potatoes evenly onto the baking sheet.
7. Sprinkle any leftover spices atop the sweet potatoes.
8. Bake on the center rack of your oven for 20-22 minutes.
9. Remove from the oven and serve warm.

36

calories	fats(g)	carbs(g)	protein(g)
124	0	23	8

 4 servings

Balsamic Roasted Brussels Sprouts

Ingredients

1.5 lbs brussels sprouts

spray oil

2 tbsp balsamic vinegar

1 tbsp Swerve brown sugar

2 tsp garlic powder

salt and pepper to taste

Method

1. Preheat your oven to 425F.
2. Trim brussels sprouts, removing any loose leaves from the outside. Slice in half, lengthwise.
3. In a large bowl add the vinegar, brown sugar and garlic powder. Mix until combined.
4. Add the brussels sprouts to the bowl and toss to mix with the marinade.
5. Line a baking sheet with foil and spread your brussels sprouts evenly onto the baking sheet.
6. Sprinkle any leftover marinade atop the brussels sprouts
7. Bake on the center rack of your oven for 20-22 minutes.
8. Remove from the oven and serve warm.

 4 servings

1 serving = 1/2 cup cooked rice

calories	fats(g)	carbs(g)	protein(g)
186	1	38	7

Protein Jasmine Rice

Ingredients

1 cup jasmine rice, dry

2 cups bone broth

1 tsp salt

Method

1. In a medium saucepan, over medium heat, bring 1 cup of jasmine rice, 1 tsp of salt and 2 cups of bone broth to a boil. Lower heat to simmer, cover and cook for 18 minutes or until rice is tender and all broth is absorbed.

2 servings

calories	fats(g)	carbs(g)	protein(g)
70	2	10	3

Air Fried Green Beans

Ingredients

1 lb fresh green beans

1/4 cup grated parmesan cheese

1 tbsp garlic powder

salt & pepper to taste

spray oil

Method

1. Preheat your air fryer to 380F.
2. Place the green beans in a large bowl and spray generously with spray oil.
3. Toss the green beans with parmesan cheese, garlic powder, salt, and pepper until all green beans are well coated.
4. Place the green beans into an air fryer basket and air fry for 7-8 minutes tossing midway. The green beans should be tender and slightly browned. Work in batches when air frying the green beans. You want a single layer of green beans in your air fryer.
5. Remove from air fryer and serve warm.

calories	fats(g)	carbs(g)	protein(g)
90	6	6	3

Cucumber Tomato Feta Salad

Ingredients

2 medium sized cucumbers

20 red grape tomatoes

20 yellow grape tomatoes

1/4 red onion, sliced

1/2 cup reduced fat feta

salt and pepper to taste

1/4 cup low calorie Greek dressing

    * I use Kraft Greek dressing

    (50 calories per serving)

Method

1. Dice cucumber into 1/2 inch pieces and add to a large bowl.
2. Add grape tomatoes sliced in half, and sliced red onion.
3. Add feta cheese and 1/4 cup Greek dressing and toss to combine.
4. Serve cold.

THANK YOU

[Instagram] thecaloriedeficitqueen

[TikTok] thecaloriedeficitqueen

[YouTube] @thecaloriedeficitqueen3134

You can find more of my low calorie
Ecookbooks at
https://payhip.com/4Mfit

Thank you so much for purchasing this e-book! I love creating low calorie recipes to help keep you in a calorie deficit and allow you to eat like a queen! I hope you love it and enjoy the meals for many years to come. Please feel free to contact me at any time with questions via my email 4Mfitusa@gmail.com.

Kacy

4MFiT

Made in the USA
Las Vegas, NV
21 July 2023

75076436R00026